GCSE English Literature
Revise
Dr Jekyll & Mr Hyde
Model Answers and Practice
from
GCSEEnglish.uk

Edward Mooney

gcseenglish.uk

Copyright © 2023 by Edward Mooney

All rights reserved. This book or any portion thereof may not be reproduced or used in any manner whatsoever without the express written permission of the publisher except for the use of brief quotations in a book review or scholarly journal.

First Printing: 2023

ISBN 979-8366622219

www.gcseenglish.uk

Contents

Introduction	**1**
1: Frightening outsider	**5**
2: Mystery and fear	**11**
3: Scientific ambitions	**17**
4: Sympathy for Jekyll	**23**
5: Mystery and tension	**29**
6: Inhuman and disturbing	**35**
7: Good and evil	**41**
8: Disturbing and threatening	**47**
9: Duality of man	**53**
10: Investigation	**59**
11: Friendship	**63**
12: Science	**69**
Appendix 1: How will my essay be assessed?	**73**
Appendix 2: Endnotes	**76**

Introduction

In this book, you will find the guidance you need to help you improve your AQA GCSE English Literature essays on *The Strange Case of Dr Jekyll and Mr Hyde* (hereafter referred to as *Jekyll and Hyde*).

There are practice exam-style essay tasks, essay writing checklists and complete full-marks model answers to help show you what a good essay looks like and what the examiners are looking for. All the tasks are based on recent, publicly available past papers.

Essay writing is a very important part of the English curriculum and is assessed extensively at GCSE; the AQA *Jekyll and Hyde* assessment represents 19% of your total GCSE English Literature grade. Regular practice of essay writing is therefore vital for boosting exam grades.

Regular essay writing practice will also help improve your knowledge of the text.

How to use this book

There are a range of different ways you can use this book. You could:

- read the essays and see what an excellent exam answer looks like.
- read the exam tasks and then plan and write your own essays.
- use the checklists (provided after every essay) to see how many of the writing recommendations are met by each essay.
- use the checklists (provided after every essay) to help you plan and write your own essays.
- read the essays again, more slowly, identifying, and remembering, key interpretations of *Jekyll and Hyde*.
- re-write the essays using different textual evidence and/or a differing set of interpretations.

Of course, these are practice tasks and model answers. Your writing in your exam should be your own work. Don't attempt to memorise an essay and copy it out as you risk being penalised, such as having marks taken away or even being disqualified from the entire exam.

About Interpretation of Text and Context

Interpretation of literary texts and contexts can differ from person to person. Thus, you may read interpretations here that are new to you or perhaps you may even disagree with some of them. This is to be expected as literary texts are open to interpretation, and interpretations often change radically over time, leading to the existence of differing, apparently contradictory interpretations. Understandably, this can lead students to feel uncertainty about which interpretations are best for use in exam essays.

My solution to this is to stay close to the mainstream interpretations. On the whole, the interpretations you will read here are widely found in revision guides, textbooks and online study aids. I have also made extensive use of the interpretations identified as top band indicative content in exam board mark schemes, exemplars and training material. My reasonable assumption is: if it is in the mark scheme then it should be in the essay.

If the mainstream interpretations change (which is entirely possible), then I will update the essays in future editions.

Learning about the less mainstream interpretations, while fascinating, is proper for A Level students and higher. The assessment objectives at GCSE do not ask for 'other interpretations' as is common on A Level exam specifications. (See Appendix 1 for more information on assessment objectives.)

Having noted all this, if you feel inspired to dig deeper into the complex world of different interpretations of the text and context, and you have the time to do so, please do.

A Note on the Text

There are many different editions of the text. I have used the version below:

- *Dr Jekyll and Mr Hyde: with The Merry Men & Other Stories (Wordsworth Classics)*. ISBN: 978-1853260612. https://amzn.to/3EsxqQY (All quotations and page references are taken from this text.)

More about me

I am a qualified teacher of English with a degree in English Literature from the University of Cambridge. I have taught and examined GCSE and A Level English courses at outstanding schools since 2006. I now write model answers and provide exam preparation through my website gcseenglish.uk.

Keep up to date with future projects and collections of model answers by subscribing to my newsletter or following my social media channels. Visit gcseenglish.uk or search gcseenglishuk and feel free to leave a review.

Best of luck in your exams!

1: Frightening outsider

Read the following extract from Chapter 2 (Search for Mr Hyde) of *The Strange Case of Dr Jekyll and Mr Hyde* and then answer the question that follows.

In this extract Mr Utterson has just met Mr Hyde for the first time.

> "We have common friends," said Mr Utterson.
>
> "Common friends!" echoed Mr Hyde, a little hoarsely. "Who are they?"
>
> "Jekyll, for instance," said the lawyer.
>
> "He never told you," cried Mr Hyde, with a flush of anger. "I did not think you would have lied.'"
>
> "Come," said Mr Utterson, "that is not fitting language."
>
> The other snarled aloud into a savage laugh; and the next moment, with extraordinary quickness, he had unlocked the door and disappeared into the house.
>
> The lawyer stood awhile when Mr Hyde had left him, the picture of disquietude. Then he began slowly to mount the street, pausing every step or two and putting his hand to his brow like a man in mental perplexity. The problem he was thus debating as he walked was one of a class that is rarely solved. Mr Hyde was pale and dwarfish; he gave an impression of deformity without any nameable malformation, he had a displeasing smile, he had borne himself to the lawyer with a sort of murderous mixture of timidity and boldness, and he spoke with a husky whispering and somewhat broken voice, – all these were points against him; but not all of these together could explain the hitherto unknown disgust, loathing and fear with which Mr Utterson regarded him. "There must be something else," said the perplexed gentleman. "There is something more, if I could find a name for it. God bless me, the man seems hardly human! Something troglodytic, shall we say? Or can it be the old story of Dr Fell? Or is it the mere radiance of a foul soul that thus transpires through, and transfigures, its clay continent? The last, I think; for, O my poor old Harry Jekyll, if ever I read Satan's signature upon a face, it is on that of your new friend!"

Starting with this extract, how does Stevenson present Mr Hyde as a frightening outsider?

Write about:

- how Stevenson presents Mr Hyde in this extract
- how Stevenson presents Mr Hyde as a frightening outsider in the novel as a whole.

1: The Essay

In *Jekyll and Hyde*, Stevenson shows how Hyde's immoral behaviour leads those he encounters to reject him as a frightening outsider. Utterson, in particular, is repulsed by Hyde but struggles to understand exactly why. His choice of language betrays his disgust and shows that he feels Hyde is an outsider, taking advantage, he believes, of that pillar of the establishment, Dr Jekyll. Ultimately, we learn that Hyde is in fact Dr Jekyll and is, therefore, an 'insider', leaving us with the troubling sense that even ostensibly respectable people may hide shocking secrets.

In the extract, Stevenson presents Utterson reacting with fright and disgust at his first meeting with Hyde. Their meeting ends with Hyde "snarl[ing]...a savage laugh," (p11) a sneering response to Utterson's condemnation of Hyde's 'un-gentlemanly' attitude. The metaphor suggests that Hyde is a wild animal and also echoes Victorian prejudices about Indigenous peoples, who were dismissed as 'uncivilised' 'savages'. After the encounter, Utterson strives to understand his viscerally negative reaction to Hyde, who he feels is "deform[ed]." (p12) Utterson's use of pseudo-scientific terminology shows that he believes Hyde must be disabled somehow, again betraying his prejudices, leading him to use a tricolon to emphasise his "disgust, loathing and fear." (p12) Stevenson then shows Utterson's ruminations continuing as he bombards himself with questions, wondering if Hyde is variously "hardly human," "troglodytic," or a "foul soul" marked by "Satan." (p12) Utterson is grasping desperately for an explanation, wondering if Hyde is inhuman, or an 'unevolved' cave-dweller, or a servant of the devil. All show that Utterson comprehensively rejects Hyde, believing him to be a sinful outsider who cannot be tolerated in 'civilised' society.

Earlier in the novel, Stevenson presents Enfield's shocked testimony which immediately positions Hyde as an outsider figure. Enfield narrates Hyde, "like some damned Juggernaut," (p5) trampling over a young girl. The simile others Hyde, associating him with a Hindu festival and suggesting that he is somehow exotic and dangerous, a non-Christian outsider in a generally Christian society.[1] As with Utterson, Enfield's Euro-centric prejudices, widespread in the Victorian era at the height of European imperialism, are clear, and he continues to display them when he describes Hyde's "black sneering coolness" (p5) and contrasts him with Dr Jekyll who is "the very pink of the proprieties." (p6) The colour imagery sets up a pattern of dark and light contrasts in the novel and also suggests that Enfield reacts to Hyde as a racial inferior, someone to be feared and condemned.

Moreover, Stevenson uses the setting of Victorian London to emphasise Hyde's outsider status. Enfield remarks that the location of Hyde's crime is "sinister" and "sordid." (p4) Later, Hyde's dwelling is presented, through a dirty London fog, as a "blackguardly" (p17) slum. The fearful atmosphere echoes the traditions of Gothic literature, placing Hyde alongside Frankenstein's creature, both of whom are man-made frightening outsiders, despised and feared by their creators.

Stevenson eventually reveals that Hyde is simultaneously a frightening outsider *and* the respected 'insider', Dr Jekyll. Hyde is presented as killing "with ape-like fury" (p16) the "beautiful" (p15) Sir Danvers Carew MP. The simile again presents Hyde as an unevolved human, reflecting the late-Victorian fascination with Darwin's theory of evolution, suggesting that Hyde is more 'primitive' than 'civilised' humans. Moreover, the contrast of Hyde with an MP emphasises how Hyde's behaviour, previously affecting only impoverished outsiders, is now threatening people at the pinnacle of Victorian society – the outsider is closing in on the 'insiders'. Stevenson then presents Dr Lanyon's witnessing of Hyde's transformation into Dr Jekyll. Hyde calls the transformation an act to "stagger the unbelief of Satan." (p40) Again, the devil is invoked, suggesting Hyde's activities are evil. Indeed, Hyde seems to believe he is more powerful than Satan and revels in his unholy powers. Dr Jekyll later reveals the frightening truth – that he sought to escape the life of a "discontented doctor" (p49) and experience the "liberty" and "glee" (p49) of "depravity." (p46) Though he attempts to give a veneer of scientific respectability to his 'research', we realise that Dr Jekyll seems simply to be driven by a desire to 'go wild'. Perhaps, the truly frightening revelation, then, is that Dr Jekyll chose, *repeatedly*, to be the outsider Hyde, despite knowing the terrible truth of Hyde's actions.

Thus, Stevenson presents a wealthy establishment man taking on the guise of a frightening outsider in order to satisfy his taste for criminal pleasures. The novel, therefore, condemns the hypocrisy of those who use their riches to indulge in behaviour they would otherwise denounce as immoral. Ultimately, perhaps the most frightening aspect of the novel is the suggestion that we will always struggle to know for sure who anyone really is, behind the smiles and the carefully curated public exterior.

1: Essay Writing Checklist

As you read, check how many of the recommendations below are followed by the essay. Then, use the checklist to help you write your own essay.

Remember that these are *recommendations* from an experienced teacher, not *requirements*. Allow them to help and guide you, but don't allow them to restrict you; if you have a different idea and feel confident about it, then give it a go!

- ☐ Use wording of question in answer – "Stevenson presents."
- ☐ Use Intro and Conclusion to help structure essay as argument.
- ☐ Use topic sentences to open each main paragraph.
- ☐ Close focus on extract.
- ☐ Focus on elsewhere in the novel.
- ☐ Use short, precise quotations to support interpretations.
- ☐ Close analysis of language.
- ☐ Close analysis of form.
- ☐ Close analysis of text structure.
- ☐ Refer to effect on reader.
- ☐ Use relevant subject terminology.
- ☐ Connect to context when text was written, where relevant: late-Victorian era.
- ☐ Connect to context when text is set, where relevant: late-Victorian era.
- ☐ Connect to literary context, where relevant: history of the Gothic genre.
- ☐ Connect to original and 21st century audience context, where relevant.
- ☐ Focus on minor character(s), where relevant.
- ☐ Use accurate spelling, punctuation and grammar.
- ☐ Write c450-c750 words.

2: Mystery and fear

Read the following extract from Chapter 1 (Story of the Door) of *The Strange Case of Dr Jekyll and Mr Hyde* and then answer the question that follows.

In this extract, Utterson and Enfield are out for a walk. This walk has taken them into the area where Mr Hyde lives.

> It chanced on one of these rambles that their way led them down a by-street in a busy quarter of London. The street was small and what is called quiet, but it drove a thriving trade on the weekdays. The inhabitants were all doing well, it seemed and all emulously hoping to do better still, and laying out the surplus of their grains in coquetry; so that the shop fronts stood along that thoroughfare with an air of invitation, like rows of smiling saleswomen. Even on Sunday, when it veiled its more florid charms and lay comparatively empty of passage, the street shone out in contrast to its dingy neighbourhood, like a fire in a forest; and with its freshly painted shutters, well-polished brasses, and general cleanliness and gaiety of note, instantly caught and pleased the eye of the passenger.
>
> Two doors from one corner, on the left hand going east the line was broken by the entry of a court; and just at that point a certain sinister block of building thrust forward its gable on the street. It was two storeys high; showed no window, nothing but a door on the lower storey and a blind forehead of discoloured wall on the upper; and bore in every feature, the marks of prolonged and sordid negligence. The door, which was equipped with neither bell nor knocker, was blistered and distained. Tramps slouched into the recess and struck matches on the panels; children kept shop upon the steps; the schoolboy had tried his knife on the mouldings; and for close on a generation, no one had appeared to drive away these random visitors or to repair their ravages.

Starting with this extract, how does Stevenson use settings to create mystery and fear?

Write about:

- how Stevenson describes the setting in this extract

- how Stevenson uses settings to create mystery and fear in the novel as a whole.

2: The Essay

In *Jekyll and Hyde*, Stevenson uses contrasting settings to emphasise the mystery of the two halves of Dr Jekyll's personality. Description of pleasant London streets is juxtaposed with a Gothic-infused description of sinister backstreets, creating a sense of mystery and fear. Interior office and laboratory scenes imply honest intellectual labour but are in fact places where the grotesque truth of Dr Jekyll is revealed. Stevenson presents late-Victorian London as a character in its own right, a fearful antagonist working to destroy Dr Jekyll and put an end to his depravity.

In the extract, Stevenson presents Hyde's mysterious dwelling standing out in an otherwise ordinary street. This part of London is "thriving" (p3) and busy on weekdays with hard-working people going about their ordinary lives. The street stands out "like a fire in a forest" (p4) compared to surrounding streets, the simile suggesting beauty and "gaiety" (p4) but also threat and destruction. Perhaps, we wonder, the street may be hiding something. Indeed, Stevenson then shifts our focus to examine a mysterious building that imposes itself in this otherwise pleasant scene. The building is "sinister" (p4) and windowless suggesting that it is trying to hide something. Moreover, the building is "discoloured," "blistered" and "distained." (p4) The narrator denounces the building's state as "sordid" (p4) and, when we later learn that this is Mr Hyde's dwelling, we can infer that this neglected building reflects the grotesque immorality of its inhabitant. Immediately outside the building gather "slouch[ing]" (p4) tramps, child street pedlars and vandals. These are not the industrious traders of elsewhere on the street and suggest Dr Jekyll has 'fallen', debasing himself by becoming Hyde and consorting with people that 'good' Victorian gentlemen should strive to avoid.

Stevenson later presents this mysterious dwelling in more detail, emphasising Hyde's moral degradation. Near Hyde's house, London is presented as being dark in the daytime as the wind, "charging and routing," (p17) tries to defeat a dense fog. The personification of nature, and the military metaphors, suggest a battle between darkness and light – a battle that darkness is winning – perhaps reflecting a similar moral battle for Dr Jekyll's soul. Utterson is then presented as recoiling, considering the area to be "like a district of some city in a nightmare." (p17) The simile reflects that fact that a Victorian gentleman such as Utterson would not usually enter these streets, preferring instead to live a life of ignorant wealth, never confronted with the 'nightmarish' truth of poverty. Indeed,

Utterson's prejudice is further emphasised when he shows his disgust at "blackguardly" (p17) scenes of impoverished women out for "a morning glass." (p17) The mystery, for Utterson, is why Dr Jekyll, a multi-millionaire (in today's money),[2] would choose to befriend someone living in this place, surrounded by foreign alcoholics. As was common among wealthy Victorians, poverty is understood by Utterson as a moral failing rather than an institutional failure or a lack of charity, and he condemns Dr Jekyll for not having better taste in friends.

Stevenson extends his use of fearful Gothic elements and mysterious patterns of contrasts to his presentation of the interior settings of the novel. Dr Jekyll's laboratory is presented as a "dingy windowless structure" (p19) that once was busy with students but now lies "gaunt and silent." (p19) The contrast between its previous beneficial use and its current malign use reinforces our sense that Dr Jekyll has turned decisively away from leading a 'genteel' life, towards a life of depravity. Contrasts continue when Stevenson presents Utterson's rooms to us. They are welcoming and cosy, "gay with firelight," (p21) and wine is presented as "disperse[ing] the fogs of London." (p21) The fearful sense of London as a place of horror is dispelled for a moment, suggesting that Utterson is a good man, fighting for his friend and bravely seeking the truth. By contrast, when Utterson breaks into Dr Jekyll's cabinet and sees Hyde's dying body, the fire is not presented as cosy and happy. Instead "the fire sparkl[es] in a hundred repetitions" (p34) turning Dr Jekyll's cabinet into a vision of an inferno, perhaps suggesting the fearful image of eternal damnation that awaits him in Hell.

Thus, Stevenson uses the settings to emphasise the fearful contrasts in Dr Jekyll's dual character. The descriptions of fog-bound London impart a Gothic sense of mystery and fear to the story and the rare shafts of daylight fail to dispel the gloom. Even inside Dr Jekyll's dwelling, Stevenson presents a mysterious world of terrifying science far from the benevolent medicine that Dr Jekyll should be practising. Only the cosy, quiet interior of Utterson's dwelling emphasises moral goodness, suggesting that Utterson's loyal, honourable, temperate demeanour is the antidote to Dr Jekyll's poison.

2: Essay Writing Checklist

As you read, check how many of the recommendations below are followed by the essay. Then, use the checklist to help you write your own essay.

Remember that these are *recommendations* from an experienced teacher, not *requirements*. Allow them to help and guide you, but don't allow them to restrict you; if you have a different idea and feel confident about it, then give it a go!

- ☐ Use wording of question in answer – "Stevenson presents."
- ☐ Use Intro and Conclusion to help structure essay as argument.
- ☐ Use topic sentences to open each main paragraph.
- ☐ Close focus on extract.
- ☐ Focus on elsewhere in the novel.
- ☐ Use short, precise quotations to support interpretations.
- ☐ Close analysis of language.
- ☐ Close analysis of form.
- ☐ Close analysis of text structure.
- ☐ Refer to effect on reader.
- ☐ Use relevant subject terminology.
- ☐ Connect to context when text was written, where relevant: late-Victorian era.
- ☐ Connect to context when text is set, where relevant: late-Victorian era.
- ☐ Connect to literary context, where relevant: history of the Gothic genre.
- ☐ Connect to original and 21st century audience context, where relevant.
- ☐ Focus on minor character(s), where relevant.
- ☐ Use accurate spelling, punctuation and grammar.
- ☐ Write c450-c750 words.

3: Scientific ambitions

Read the following extract from Chapter 9 (Dr Lanyon's Narrative) of *The Strange Case of Dr Jekyll and Mr Hyde* and then answer the question that follows.

In this extract, Mr Hyde speaks first. He is about to drink the potion in front of Dr Lanyon.

> "And now," said he, "to settle what remains. Will you be wise? will you be guided? will you suffer me to take this glass in my hand and to go forth from your house without further parley? or has the greed of curiosity too much command of you? Think before you answer, for it shall be done as you decide. As you decide, you shall be left as you were before, and neither richer nor wiser, unless the sense of service rendered to a man in mortal distress may be counted as a kind of riches of the soul. Or, if you shall so prefer to choose, a new province of knowledge and new avenues to fame and power shall be laid open to you, here, in this room, upon the instant; and your sight shall be blasted by a prodigy to stagger the unbelief of Satan."
>
> "Sir" said I, affecting a coolness that I was far from truly possessing, "you speak enigmas, and you will perhaps not wonder that I hear you with no very strong impression of belief. But I have gone too far in the way of inexplicable services to pause before I see the end."
>
> "It is well," replied my visitor. "Lanyon, you remember your vows: what follows is under the seal of our profession. And now, you who have so long been bound to the most narrow and material views, you who have denied the virtue of transcendental medicine, you who have derided your superiors – behold!"
>
> He put the glass to his lips and drank at one gulp. A cry followed; he reeled, staggered, clutched at the table and held on, staring with injected eyes, gasping with open mouth; and as I looked there came, I thought, a change – he seemed to swell – his face became suddenly black and the features seemed to melt and alter – and the next moment I had sprung to my feet and leaped back against the wall, my arm raised to shield me from that prodigy, my mind submerged in terror.

> "O God!" I screamed, and "O God!" again and again; for there before my eyes – pale and shaken, and half fainting, and groping before him with his hands, like a man restored from death – there stood Henry Jekyll!

Starting with this extract, explore how Stevenson presents the effects of Jekyll's scientific ambitions.

Write about:

- how Stevenson presents the effects of Jekyll's scientific ambitions in this extract
- how Stevenson presents the effects of Jekyll's scientific ambitions in the novel as a whole.

3: The Essay

In *Jekyll and Hyde*, Stevenson presents the horrifying consequences of Dr Jekyll's scientific ambitions. Rather than pursuing science for benevolent ends, Dr Jekyll instead rampages through London as Mr Hyde, leaving death and destruction in his wake. Dr Jekyll is presented as being proud of his achievements, mocking the materialist science of Dr Lanyon and revelling in depravity. Ultimately, however, Stevenson shows that Dr Jekyll's scientific ambitions lead him only to his doom.

In the extract, Stevenson reveals the horrifying effect of Dr Jekyll's scientific research. Hyde is presented sneering at Lanyon's lack of ambition and offering, after a flurry of taunting rhetorical questions, to "stagger the unbelief of Satan." (p40) The religious allusion shows that Hyde believes himself to be more evil than Satan and his blasphemous pride in such a belief would have been profoundly shocking to many of the original readers of the novel. Hyde then builds suspense with continued taunting, emphasised by anaphora and tricolon ("you who have"), (p41) ending with the imperative "behold!" (p41) Hyde is presented as a showman, enjoying the opportunity to demonstrate his previously secret scientific findings to his professional rival. Moreover, "behold," a word used repeatedly in the King James Bible, often spoken by God,[3] suggests that Hyde sees himself as taking God's place. As Lanyon witnesses the transformation, he is "submerged in terror." (p41) The metaphor suggests drowning and readers too, finally confronted with the truth after many subtle clues and misinterpretations, share Lanyon's horror. Stevenson offers no hope in this scene, presenting Dr Jekyll's scientific ambition as a grotesque abomination that shakes the very foundations of Victorian culture.

Earlier in the novel, Stevenson presents Hyde's behaviour as a negative effect of Dr Jekyll's scientific ambitions. Enfield narrates Hyde, "like some damned Juggernaut," (p5) trampling over a young girl. The simile others Hyde, associating him with a Hindu festival and suggesting that this product of Dr Jekyll's scientific ambition is somehow exotic and dangerous, a non-Christian outsider in a generally Christian society. Subsequently, Utterson's first encounter with Hyde leads him to describe Hyde as "troglodytic" and a "foul soul" marked by "Satan." (p12) This suggests that Hyde as an 'unevolved' cave-dweller, a disturbing primitive human, in league with the devil, with immoral, 'uncivilised' urges. Later, Hyde is presented as killing Sir Danvers Carew "with ape-like fury." (p16) The simile again presents Hyde as an unevolved human, reflecting the late-Victorian fascination with Darwin's theory of evolution, suggesting that Hyde is more 'primitive' than 'civilised' humans. Stevenson thus suggests that Dr Jekyll's scientific ambitions lead only to depravity, death and destruction.

In the final chapter, Stevenson presents Dr Jekyll's first person justification of his scientific experimentation. Dr Jekyll argues that his dual nature, both enjoying the "furtherance of knowledge" and being "plunged in shame," (p42) leads him to hypothesise the "mist-like transience" (p43) of our physical selves. Dr Jekyll's simile emphasises his belief that the human self is not solid but in fact "radically" (p42) dual. From a twenty-first century perspective, Dr Jekyll's conjecture does not appear shocking as post-modern theories argue that we are able to 'perform' multiple versions of our 'selves' in a world of ever-changing narratives. However, Dr Jekyll then argues that our dual natures should be separated to allow this "curse of mankind," (p43) our duality, to be lifted. Dr Jekyll appears unwilling to acknowledge that this hypothesis implies that we live in a world of radically evil people, unrestrained by their other, more moral, nature. In fact, Dr Jekyll later reveals that, as Hyde, he thoroughly enjoyed the "liberty" and "glee" (p49) of "depravity" (p46) and, ultimately, lost control of the transformation process. Having attempted to give a veneer of scientific respectability to his 'research', Dr Jekyll now seems to admit that he was driven by a desire to 'go wild'. Readers may well reject Dr Jekyll's justifications for his actions and interpret his scientific ambitions simply as the action of a wealthy man using his money to attempt to satisfy his lusts undetected.

Thus, Stevenson presents the horrifying and violent effects of Dr Jekyll's scientific ambition. Moreover, the implications of Dr Jekyll's findings – science should liberate humans from moral goodness to allow us to be truly free – are chilling, and presage later extremist ideologies.[4] Ultimately, Stevenson does not allay any late-Victorian anxieties about the deleterious effects of scientific progress so, as long as individuals are driven by ambition in the same way Dr Jekyll is, we may always need to be alert to the ways science can be perverted and put to malign use.

3: Essay Writing Checklist

As you read, check how many of the recommendations below are followed by the essay. Then, use the checklist to help you write your own essay.

Remember that these are *recommendations* from an experienced teacher, not *requirements*. Allow them to help and guide you, but don't allow them to restrict you; if you have a different idea and feel confident about it, then give it a go!

- [ ] Use wording of question in answer – "Stevenson presents."
- [ ] Use Intro and Conclusion to help structure essay as argument.
- [ ] Use topic sentences to open each main paragraph.
- [ ] Close focus on extract.
- [ ] Focus on elsewhere in the novel.
- [ ] Use short, precise quotations to support interpretations.
- [ ] Close analysis of language.
- [ ] Close analysis of form.
- [ ] Close analysis of text structure.
- [ ] Refer to effect on reader.
- [ ] Use relevant subject terminology.
- [ ] Connect to context when text was written, where relevant: late-Victorian era.
- [ ] Connect to context when text is set, where relevant: late-Victorian era.
- [ ] Connect to literary context, where relevant: history of the Gothic genre.
- [ ] Connect to original and 21st century audience context, where relevant.
- [ ] Focus on minor character(s), where relevant.
- [ ] Use accurate spelling, punctuation and grammar.
- [ ] Write c450-c750 words.

4: Sympathy for Jekyll

Read the following extract from Chapter 7 (Incident at the Window) of *The Strange Case of Dr Jekyll and Mr Hyde* and then answer the question that follows.

In this extract, Mr Utterson and Mr Enfield are talking to Dr Jekyll through his window.

> The court was very cool and a little damp, and full of premature twilight, although the sky, high up overhead, was still bright with sunset. The middle one of the three windows was half-way open; and sitting close beside it, taking the air with an infinite sadness of mien, like some disconsolate prisoner, Utterson saw Dr Jekyll.
>
> "What! Jekyll!" he cried. "I trust you are better."
>
> "I am very low, Utterson," replied the doctor drearily, "very low. It will not last long, thank God."
>
> "You stay too much indoors," said the lawyer. "You should be out, whipping up the circulation like Mr. Enfield and me. (This is my cousin—Mr. Enfield—Dr Jekyll.) Come now; get your hat and take a quick turn with us."
>
> "You are very good," sighed the other. "I should like to very much; but no, no, no, it is quite impossible; I dare not. But indeed, Utterson, I am very glad to see you; this is really a great pleasure; I would ask you and Mr. Enfield up, but the place is really not fit."
>
> "Why then," said the lawyer good-naturedly, "the best thing we can do is to stay down here and speak with you from where we are."
>
> "That is just what I was about to venture to propose," returned the doctor, with a smile. But the words were hardly uttered, before the smile was struck out of his face and succeeded by an expression of such abject terror and despair as froze the very blood of the two gentlemen below. They saw it but for a glimpse, for the window was instantly thrust down; but that glimpse had been sufficient, and they turned and left the court without a word.

'Stevenson's presentation of Dr Jekyll allows the reader to feel sympathy for him.'

Starting with this extract, explore how far you agree with this opinion.

Write about:
- how Stevenson presents Dr Jekyll in this extract
- how Stevenson presents Dr Jekyll in the novel as a whole.

4: The Essay

In *Jekyll and Hyde,* Stevenson does indeed generate sympathy for Dr Jekyll who is presented as being a pillar of society working hard to develop useful scientific knowledge. Stevenson shows him resisting his transformations into Hyde, despising who he becomes and eventually committing suicide in order to kill Hyde. However, there are elements of Dr Jekyll's story with which readers may struggle to sympathise; instead, we may reject his behaviour as selfish, criminal and evil.

In the extract, Stevenson creates sympathy for Dr Jekyll by showing that he is unable to control transformation into Hyde. Stevenson creates a contrast between the bright sky overhead and the "premature twilight" (p25) of the court in which sits Dr Jekyll "like some disconsolate prisoner." (p26) The simile suggests that Jekyll is not only imprisoned physically, unable to leave for fear (as we later learn) of transforming into Hyde, but also psychologically, held in thrall to his horrifying alter ego. The short dialogue between the despondent Dr Jekyll and his hearty friends emphasises Dr Jekyll's withdrawal into darkness, and his rejection of Utterson's invitation, "I dare not," (p26) suggests that he's afraid of something, or someone. Subsequently, the horror of the transformation elicits sympathy for Dr Jekyll. His "smile was struck out of his face," (p26) and was replaced by "abject terror and despair" which "froze the very blood" (p26) of Utterson and Enfield. The metaphors are dramatic and aggressive emphasising just how violent a change we have just witnessed. Like Dr Jekyll's friends, we are perplexed and may indeed feel a deep sense of sympathy for a very unwell man.

However, it is difficult to feel much sympathy for Dr Jekyll after witnessing the horror of Mr Hyde. Enfield narrates his witnessing of Hyde who "trampled calmly" (p4) over a young girl. The jarring oxymoron emphasises Hyde's lack of compassion and, chillingly, suggests that trampling pedestrians to death is a regular occurrence for Hyde who blithely offers to pay c£10,000 in modern terms[5] in order to avoid arrest. Later in the novel, Hyde's murder of Sir Danvers Carew is horrifying. Hyde beats the MP until his bones are "audibly shattered." (p16) The imagery is viscerally shocking and readers may now struggle to feel sympathy for a brutal murderer. Later, when Stevenson presents Hyde's transformation into Dr Jekyll, we hear the sneering arrogance that motivates Hyde. He calls his transformation an act to "stagger the unbelief of Satan." (p40) The invocation of the devil suggests that Hyde's activities are evil. Indeed, Hyde seems to believe he is more powerful than Satan and revels in his unholy powers. Few original readers, mostly Victorian Christians, and few twenty-first century readers, can react sympathetically to such immoral hubris.

Stevenson later creates some sympathy for Dr Jekyll as we read his first person statement. Dr Jekyll argues that his research began with good intentions, aiming for the "furtherance of knowledge," (p42) leading him to hypothesise the "mist-like transience" (p43) of our physical selves. Dr Jekyll's simile emphasises his belief that the human self is not solid but in fact "radically" (p42) dual and, from a twenty-first century perspective, Dr Jekyll's conjecture appears plausible as post-modern theories argue that we are able to 'perform' multiple versions of our 'selves' in a world of ever-changing narratives. However, our sympathy starts to dissipate when Dr Jekyll argues that our dual natures should be separated to allow this "curse of mankind," (p43) our duality, to be lifted. Dr Jekyll appears unwilling to acknowledge that his hypothesis posits a world of radically evil people, unrestrained by their other, more moral, nature. In fact, Dr Jekyll later reveals that, as Hyde, he thoroughly enjoyed the "liberty" and "glee" (p49) of "depravity." (p46) Stevenson here presents Dr Jekyll as a transgressive gothic hero, driven by a desire to go beyond the restrictive boundaries of Victorian morality. At this point, readers may well cease to have sympathy for Dr Jekyll, even after his suicide, as we interpret his behaviour as the actions of a selfish man using his wealth to satisfy his immoral lusts undetected.

Thus, Stevenson presents readers with a dilemma: sympathy or condemnation. It is true that we can sympathise with Dr Jekyll's genuine attempts to resist his transformations; we can sympathise with his addiction, to the potion, to Hyde, to the glee of depravity. We can also sympathise with him as a victim of suicide. Ultimately, though, it is hard to see past Hyde's crimes. Though we only witness two criminal acts, many more are alluded to, and it is clear that Hyde has terrorised the people of London for years who, we may infer, would be very happy to hear of his demise.

4: Essay Writing Checklist

As you read, check how many of the recommendations below are followed by the essay. Then, use the checklist to help you write your own essay.

Remember that these are *recommendations* from an experienced teacher, not *requirements*. Allow them to help and guide you, but don't allow them to restrict you; if you have a different idea and feel confident about it, then give it a go!

- [ ] Use wording of question in answer – "Stevenson presents."
- [ ] Use Intro and Conclusion to help structure essay as argument.
- [ ] Use topic sentences to open each main paragraph.
- [ ] Close focus on extract.
- [ ] Focus on elsewhere in the novel.
- [ ] Use short, precise quotations to support interpretations.
- [ ] Close analysis of language.
- [ ] Close analysis of form.
- [ ] Close analysis of text structure.

- [ ] Refer to effect on reader.
- [ ] Use relevant subject terminology.
- [ ] Connect to context when text was written, where relevant: late-Victorian era.
- [ ] Connect to context when text is set, where relevant: late-Victorian era.
- [ ] Connect to literary context, where relevant: history of the Gothic genre.
- [ ] Connect to original and 21st century audience context, where relevant.
- [ ] Focus on minor character(s), where relevant.
- [ ] Use accurate spelling, punctuation and grammar.
- [ ] Write c450-c750 words.

5: Mystery and tension

Read the following extract from Chapter 4 (The Carew Murder Case) of *The Strange Case of Dr Jekyll and Mr Hyde* and then answer the question that follows.

In this extract, Utterson and Inspector Newcomen have come to find Mr Hyde at his lodging house after the murder of Sir Danvers Carew.

> It was by this time about nine in the morning, and the first fog of the season. A great chocolate-coloured pall lowered over heaven, but the wind was continually charging and routing these embattled vapours; so that as the cab crawled from street to street, Mr. Utterson beheld a marvellous number of degrees and hues of twilight; for here it would be dark like the back-end of evening; and there would be a glow of a rich, lurid brown, like the light of some strange conflagration; and here, for a moment, the fog would be quite broken up, and a haggard shaft of daylight would glance in between the swirling wreaths. The dismal quarter of Soho seen under these changing glimpses, with its muddy ways, and slatternly passengers, and its lamps, which had never been extinguished or had been kindled afresh to combat this mournful re-invasion of darkness, seemed, in the lawyer's eyes, like a district of some city in a nightmare.
>
> The thoughts of his mind, besides, were of the gloomiest dye; and when he glanced at the companion of his drive, he was conscious of some touch of that terror of the law and the law's officers which may at times assail the most honest.
>
> As the cab drew up before the address indicated, the fog lifted a little, and showed him a dingy street, a gin-palace, a low French eating-house, a shop for the retail of penny numbers and twopenny salads, many ragged children huddled in the doorways, and many women of many different nationalities passing out, key in hand, to have a morning glass; and the next moment the fog settled down again upon that part, as brown as umber, and cut him off from his blackguardly surroundings. This was the home of Henry Jekyll's favourite; of a man who was heir to a quarter of a million sterling.

Starting with this extract, explore how Stevenson creates mystery and tension in *The Strange Case of Dr Jekyll and Mr Hyde*.

Write about:
- how Stevenson creates mystery and tension in this extract
- how Stevenson creates mystery and tension in the novel as a whole.

5: The Essay

In *Jekyll and Hyde*, Stevenson tells the mysterious story of the connection between a respected doctor and a grotesquely immoral murderer. Stevenson presents Utterson as the investigator who gathers evidence in an attempt to solve the mystery. Tension rises, emphasised by the eerie setting, as Hyde's crimes escalate and Dr Jekyll retreats from society. Ultimately, the mystery is so complex that Utterson is unable to resolve it and readers have to wait for Dr Jekyll's confession to understand the truth.

In the extract, Stevenson creates mystery and tension by presenting London as a gothic landscape of darkness and danger. Near Hyde's house, London is dark in the daytime as the wind, "charging and routing," (p17) tries to defeat a dense fog. The personification of nature, and the military metaphors, suggest a tense battle between darkness and light – a battle that darkness is winning – perhaps reflecting a similar moral battle for Dr Jekyll's soul. Utterson is then presented as recoiling with fear, considering the area to be "like a district of some city in a nightmare." (p17) The simile raises the tension of the scene, suggesting that Utterson is arriving at a place of danger where mysterious things may happen, hidden by the dense fog. Utterson is then presented as being mystified and disgusted by "blackguardly" (p17) scenes of impoverished women out for "a morning glass." (p17) The mystery, for Utterson, is why Dr Jekyll, a multi-millionaire in today's money,[6] would choose to befriend someone living in this place, surrounded by foreign alcoholics. As was common among wealthy Victorians, poverty is understood by Utterson as a moral failing and so the moral degradation of a scene like this would be felt by the original readers as threat to their morality, serving to increase the tension.

Elsewhere in the novel, Stevenson creates mystery and tension through the depiction of Hyde's awful crimes. Enfield's narrative presents Hyde as a mysterious, horrifying figure who, "like some damned Juggernaut," (p5) tramples over a young girl. The simile others Hyde, associating him with a Hindu festival and suggesting, mysteriously, that he is somehow exotic and dangerous, a non-Christian outsider in a generally Christian society. Later, tension in the plot rises as Hyde escalates from assault to murder, killing Sir Danvers Carew "with ape-like fury." (p16) The simile presents Hyde as an unevolved human, reflecting the late-Victorian fascination with Darwin's theory of evolution, mysteriously suggesting that Hyde is more 'primitive' than 'civilised' humans. The mystery of

Jekyll's connection to Hyde is partly resolved by Lanyon's narration of Hyde's transformation into Dr Jekyll. In a tense stand-off with Lanyon, Hyde calls the transformation an act to "stagger the unbelief of Satan." (p40) This invocation of the devil, suggests that Hyde's behaviour is truly evil and shows that he revels in his unholy powers. Tension then dissipates when Jekyll's body is found; however, the mystery of how and why Jekyll became Hyde remains.

In the final chapter, Stevenson resolves some of this mystery through Dr Jekyll's first person justification of his behaviour. Dr Jekyll argues that he has discovered the "mist-like transience" (p43) of our bodies, the simile emphasising his belief that the human self is not solid but in fact "radically" (p42) dual. From a twenty-first century perspective, Dr Jekyll's conjecture does not appear shocking as post-modern theories argue that we are able to 'perform' multiple versions of our 'selves' in a world of ever-changing narratives. For Victorian readers, on the other hand, the hypothesis may well have been shocking, even blasphemous, and certainly mysterious. Stevenson then presents Dr Jekyll resolving the mystery further when he later reveals that, as Hyde, he thoroughly enjoyed the "liberty" and "glee" (p49) of "depravity," (p46) thus admitting that he was driven by a desire to 'go wild'. Though the mystery of Jekyll's connection to Hyde has been resolved, readers may well remain mystified at Dr Jekyll's tortured justifications for his actions, interpreting his behaviour simply as the actions of a wealthy man using his money to satisfy his lusts undetected.

Thus Stevenson creates a mysterious and tense story of a well-regarded doctor living out his dark fantasies. Set in a gothic-infused London landscape of fog and dilapidation, tension rises as the crimes escalate and the investigators close in on the truth. Ultimately, though Dr Jekyll's statement provides some resolution, one mystery remains: why is it that he chose, *repeatedly*, to be Hyde, despite knowing the terrible truth of Hyde's actions? Readers are left with the troubling implication that evil-doers choose, and enjoy, evil.

5: Essay Writing Checklist

As you read, check how many of the recommendations below are followed by the essay. Then, use the checklist to help you write your own essay.

Remember that these are *recommendations* from an experienced teacher, not *requirements*. Allow them to help and guide you, but don't allow them to restrict you; if you have a different idea and feel confident about it, then give it a go!

- ☐ Use wording of question in answer – "Stevenson presents."
- ☐ Use Intro and Conclusion to help structure essay as argument.
- ☐ Use topic sentences to open each main paragraph.
- ☐ Close focus on extract.
- ☐ Focus on elsewhere in the novel.
- ☐ Use short, precise quotations to support interpretations.
- ☐ Close analysis of language.
- ☐ Close analysis of form.
- ☐ Close analysis of text structure.
- ☐ Refer to effect on reader.
- ☐ Use relevant subject terminology.
- ☐ Connect to context when text was written, where relevant: late-Victorian era.
- ☐ Connect to context when text is set, where relevant: late-Victorian era.
- ☐ Connect to literary context, where relevant: history of the Gothic genre.
- ☐ Connect to original and 21st century audience context, where relevant.
- ☐ Focus on minor character(s), where relevant.
- ☐ Use accurate spelling, punctuation and grammar.
- ☐ Write c450-c750 words.

6: Inhuman and disturbing

Read the following extract from Chapter 8 (The Last Night) of *The Strange Case of Dr Jekyll and Mr Hyde* and then answer the question that follows.

In this extract Poole, Jekyll's servant, talks with Utterson about events at Jekyll's house.

> "That's it!" said Poole. "It was this way. I came suddenly into the theatre from the garden. It seems he had slipped out to look for this drug, or whatever it is; for the cabinet door was open, and there he was at the far end of the room digging among the crates. He looked up when I came in, gave a kind of cry, and whipped upstairs into the cabinet. It was but for one minute that I saw him, but the hair stood up on my head like quills. Sir, if that was my master, why had he a mask upon his face? If it was my master, why did he cry out like a rat, and run from me? I have served him long enough. And then …", the man paused and passed his hand over his face.
>
> "These are all very strange circumstances," said Mr. Utterson, "but I think I begin to see daylight. Your master, Poole, is plainly seized with one of those maladies that both torture and deform the sufferer; hence, for aught I know, the alteration of his voice; hence the mask and his avoidance of his friends; hence his eagerness to find this drug, by means of which the poor soul retains some hope of ultimate recovery – God grant that he be not deceived. There is my explanation; it is sad enough, Poole, ay, and appalling to consider; but it is plain and natural, hangs well together, and delivers us from all exorbitant alarms."
>
> "Sir," said the butler, turning to a sort of mottled pallor, "that thing was not my master, and there's the truth. My master" – here he looked round him and began to whisper – "is a tall, fine build of a man, and this was more of a dwarf." Utterson attempted to protest. "O sir," cried Poole, "do you think I do not know my master after twenty years? do you think I do not know where his head comes to in the cabinet door, where I saw him every morning of my life? No, sir, that thing in the mask was never Dr Jekyll – God knows what it was, but it was never Dr Jekyll; and it is the belief of my heart that there was murder done."

Starting with this extract, explore how Stevenson presents Mr Hyde as an inhuman and disturbing member of society.

Write about:

- how Stevenson presents Mr Hyde in this extract
- how Stevenson presents Mr Hyde as an inhuman and disturbing member of society in the novel as a whole.

6: The Essay

In *Jekyll and Hyde*, Stevenson presents Hyde as an inhuman and disturbing member of a society that is shocked and terrified by his behaviour. Poole rejects Utterson's attempt to rationalise Jekyll's behaviour, instead coming close to discovering the disturbing link between his employer and the inhuman creature he encounters. Elsewhere, Stevenson provides plenty of evidence of Hyde's inhuman behaviour, that takes place against the gothic backdrop of a disturbing London setting. Ultimately, we learn that Hyde is in fact Dr Jekyll, leaving us with the unsettling sense that even ostensibly respectable people may hide disturbing secrets.

In the extract, Stevenson presents how characters react to Hyde's disturbing behaviour. Poole is mystified by Hyde's secretive behaviour. His hair stands up "like quills" (p30) and his face takes on a "mottled pallor." (p30) The simile and imagery show how disturbed Poole is as he struggles to understand what he is witnessing. He wonders aloud why the person is masked and asks, "why did he cry out like a rat?" (p30) The simile presents Hyde as inhuman vermin, a hated carrier of disease, and the mask imagery emphasises how different Hyde looks, compared to Jekyll, alluding to Hyde's disturbing, secretive behaviour. Though Stevenson presents Utterson attempting to reach a rational explanation, Poole stays firm, referring to Hyde as a "thing" and "it." (p30) Using this impersonal language suggests that Poole no longer views Hyde as human, instead viewing 'it' as a mysterious disturbing figure, "more of a dwarf" (p30) than the tall, upstanding Jekyll he knows so well. Poole's disgusted response to Hyde's physical appearance reflects Victorian prejudices whereby physical 'deformity' was seen as an indication of moral 'deformity'; Poole cannot accept that such an inhuman 'thing' is a good member of society.

Earlier in the novel, Stevenson presents Hyde's disturbing and inhuman behaviour. Utterson's first encounter with Hyde leads him to describe Hyde as "troglodytic" and a "foul soul" marked by "Satan." (p12) This suggests that Utterson views Hyde as an 'unevolved' cave-dweller, a disturbing primitive human, in league with the devil, with immoral, 'uncivilised', inhuman urges. Hyde's disturbing behaviour is further emphasised by Enfield who witnesses Hyde, "like some damned Juggernaut," (p5) trampling over a young girl. The simile others Hyde, associating him with a Hindu festival and suggesting that he is somehow exotic and dangerous, a non-Christian interloper in a generally

Christian society. Later, Hyde is presented as breaking "out of all bounds" and killing Sir Danvers Carew "with ape-like fury." (p16) The simile presents Hyde as something inhuman or perhaps an unevolved human, reflecting the late-Victorian fascination with Darwin's theory of evolution, again suggesting that Hyde is more 'primitive' than 'civilised' humans. Moreover, Stevenson suggests that Hyde's transgression of the boundaries of social convention is just as disturbing for the other, very conventional, characters of the novel as his crimes.

In the final chapter, Stevenson reveals the disturbing truth about Hyde's genesis and Dr Jekyll's shocking motivation for repeatedly transforming into Hyde. Dr Jekyll argues that his dual nature, both enjoying the "furtherance of knowledge" and being "plunged in shame," (p42) leads him to hypothesise that the human self is not solid but in fact "radically" (p42) dual. Pious Victorian readers may well have been disturbed by such an assertion and its implication that 'shame' can be pleasurable. In fact, Dr Jekyll then argues that our dual natures should be separated to allow this "curse of mankind," (p43) our duality, to be lifted. Dr Jekyll appears unwilling to acknowledge that this hypothesis implies that we live in a disturbing world of radically evil people, unrestrained by their other, more moral, nature. In fact, Dr Jekyll later reveals that, as Hyde, he thoroughly enjoyed the "liberty" and "glee" (p49) of inhuman "depravity" (p46) and, ultimately, lost control of the transformation process. Having attempted to give a veneer of scientific respectability to his 'research', Dr Jekyll now seems to admit that he was driven by a desire to 'go wild'. Readers may well reject Dr Jekyll's justifications for his actions and interpret his behaviour simply as the disturbing actions of a wealthy man using his money to attempt to satisfy his lusts undetected.

Thus, Stevenson does indeed present Hyde as an inhuman, disturbing member of society. Hyde's actions are grotesque and roundly condemned by other characters as the disturbing actions of a primitive non-human, closer to an ape than a 'civilised' gentleman. Dr Jekyll's attempt to justify his choice to transform into Hyde only compounds the sense of revulsion felt by the characters, and indeed the readers. Ultimately, perhaps the most disturbing aspect of the novel is the suggestion that we will always struggle to know for sure who anyone really is, behind the smiles and the carefully curated public exterior.

6: Essay Writing Checklist

As you read, check how many of the recommendations below are followed by the essay. Then, use the checklist to help you write your own essay.

Remember that these are *recommendations* from an experienced teacher, not *requirements*. Allow them to help and guide you, but don't allow them to restrict you; if you have a different idea and feel confident about it, then give it a go!

- ☐ Use wording of question in answer – "Stevenson presents."
- ☐ Use Intro and Conclusion to help structure essay as argument.
- ☐ Use topic sentences to open each main paragraph.
- ☐ Close focus on extract.
- ☐ Focus on elsewhere in the novel.
- ☐ Use short, precise quotations to support interpretations.
- ☐ Close analysis of language.
- ☐ Close analysis of form.
- ☐ Close analysis of text structure.

- ☐ Refer to effect on reader.
- ☐ Use relevant subject terminology.
- ☐ Connect to context when text was written, where relevant: late-Victorian era.
- ☐ Connect to context when text is set, where relevant: late-Victorian era.
- ☐ Connect to literary context, where relevant: history of the Gothic genre.
- ☐ Connect to original and 21st century audience context, where relevant.
- ☐ Focus on minor character(s), where relevant.
- ☐ Use accurate spelling, punctuation and grammar.
- ☐ Write c450-c750 words.

7: Good and evil

Read the following extract from Chapter 10 (Henry Jekyll's Full Statement of the Case) of *The Strange Case of Dr Jekyll and Mr Hyde* and then answer the question that follows.

In this extract, Jekyll describes his experience of taking the potion for the first time.

> I knew myself, at the first breath of this new life, to be more wicked, tenfold more wicked, sold a slave to my original evil; and the thought, in that moment, braced and delighted me like wine. I stretched out my hands, exulting in the freshness of these sensations; and in the act I was suddenly aware that I had lost in stature.
>
> There was no mirror, at that date, in my room; that which stands beside me as I write was brought there later on, and for the very purpose of these transformations. The night, however, was far gone into the morning – the morning, black as it was, was nearly ripe for the conception of the day – the inmates of my house were locked in the most rigorous hours of slumber; and I determined, flushed as I was with hope and triumph, to venture in my new shape as far as to my bedroom. I crossed the yard, wherein the constellations looked down upon me, I could have thought, with wonder, the first creature of that sort that their unsleeping vigilance had yet disclosed to them; I stole through the corridors, a stranger in my own house; and, coming to my room, I saw for the first time the appearance of Edward Hyde.
>
> I must here speak by theory alone, saying not that which I know, but that which I suppose to be most probable. The evil side of my nature, to which I had now transferred the stamping efficacy, was less robust and less developed than the good which I had just deposed. Again, in the course of my life, which had been, after all, nine-tenths a life of effort, virtue, and control, it had been much less exercised and much less exhausted. And hence, as I think, it came about that Edward Hyde was so much smaller, slighter, and younger than Henry Jekyll. Even as good shone upon the countenance of the one, evil was written broadly and plainly on the face of the other. Evil besides (which I must still believe to be the lethal side of man) had left on that body an imprint of deformity and decay. And yet when I looked upon that ugly idol in the glass, I was conscious

> of no repugnance, rather of a leap of welcome. This too, was myself. It seemed natural and human. In my eyes it bore a livelier image of the spirit, it seemed more express and single, than the imperfect and divided countenance I had been hitherto accustomed to call mine. And in so far I was doubtless right. I have observed that when I bore the semblance of Edward Hyde, none could come near to me at first without a visible misgiving of the flesh. This, as I take it, was because all human beings, as we meet them, are commingled out of good and evil: and Edward Hyde, alone in the ranks of mankind, was pure evil.

Starting with this extract, explore how Stevenson presents ideas about good and evil in *The Strange Case of Dr Jekyll and Mr Hyde*.

Write about:
- how Stevenson presents ideas about good and evil in this extract
- how Stevenson presents ideas about good and evil in the novel as a whole.

7: The Essay

In *Jekyll and Hyde*, Stevenson suggests that life is a constant struggle against the temptations of evil. Upstanding characters in the novel strive to be good, often through immense self-abnegation. Hyde, meanwhile, is presented as being intoxicated by the joy of evil. Dr Jekyll hypothesises the concept of 'human duality' and aims to separate good from evil, but in so doing, he unleashes pure evil upon the world and is destroyed. Stevenson leaves us with the unsettling suggestion that we can all be tempted to reject lives of stultifying 'goodness' and succumb to the excitement of evil.

In the extract, Stevenson presents Dr Jekyll revelling in becoming his evil persona. Though Jekyll understands that he has become something wicked, "a slave" (p44) to evil, he confesses that this "delighted [him] like wine." (p44) The simile suggests that Jekyll feels intoxicated by evil whilst also suggesting that this is the beginning of a loss of control and a descent into moral 'slavery'. This moral degradation is emphasised by the physical transformations Jekyll notices. He has "lost in stature" (p44) and calls himself a "creature" disfigured by "deformity and decay." (p44) Hyde's shortness implies a loss in social standing by the tall Dr Jekyll; his reputation as a reputable doctor has been shattered and Hyde's physical appearance reflects his evil nature. Subsequently, Jekyll is again excited by the discovery of his dual nature and, rather than rejecting Hyde's "pure evil," (p45) Jekyll instead "welcome[s]" (p44) it. Jekyll's attitude is blasphemous and would have disturbed pious late-Victorian readers – his creation of an evil being, and his pride at his achievement, show his contempt for God and his rejection of a life of humble obedience to Jesus' teachings.

Elsewhere in the novel, Stevenson presents Hyde as a manifestation of evil. We learn that he is the evil figure who, "like some damned Juggernaut," (p5) tramples over a young girl. The simile others Hyde, associating him with a Hindu festival, thereby suggesting that his evil acts are un-Christian. Later, Hyde's evil leads to murder when he kills Sir Danvers Carew "with ape-like fury." (p16) The simile presents Hyde as an unevolved human, reflecting the late-Victorian fascination with Darwin's theory of evolution, suggesting that Hyde's evil is a result of his 'primitive' nature and implying that 'civilisation' works to control evil, allowing good to flourish. In Hyde's stand-off with Lanyon, Hyde is presented as being more evil than the devil. Hyde calls his transformation an act to "stagger the unbelief of Satan." (p40) This invocation of the devil, suggests that Hyde's behaviour is truly evil and shows that he revels in his unholy powers.

However, though evil suffuses the novel, Stevenson presents characters resisting its temptation. For example, Utterson is presented as leading an "austere" (p3) self-denying life, rejecting theatres and wine, and taking very seriously the "stringent obligations" (p25) of his profession. Utterson's self-mortification suggests that a good life must be a dull life. Ironically, Utterson's inflexible insistence on being good leads to evil – respecting Lanyon's injunction not to read his document until after Dr Jekyll's death means he misses an opportunity to save Dr Jekyll. The challenge and paradoxes of being good are explored further through Jekyll's efforts to embrace goodness. Jekyll describes his good life as that of a "discontented doctor" (p49) living a life of "severity." (p49) Again, a good life is presented as harsh and unattractive compared to the "secret pleasures" (p49) of evil. Jekyll subsequently describes himself as a "sinner" (p50) who, attempting to "redeem the past," "fell before the assaults of temptation." (p50) The metaphor presents evil as a besieging army that surrounds and then kills. Jekyll's language echoes the story of The Fall that Christians believe unleashed evil into the world.[7] He sees himself as irredeemable, another Adam, who failed to resist the temptation of knowledge and is therefore damned for eternity.

Thus, Stevenson presents evil as highly attractive, a life of joyful freedom and desire. This evil way of life tempts respectable gentlemen away from the austere moral lives they are supposed to lead, requiring incredible self-control from those who seek to lead a moral life. Dr Jekyll believes he has discovered a way to liberate good from evil but, in so doing, allows evil the freedom, un-tempered by good, to overturn social and religious convention leading only to horror and murder. Though twenty-first culture is far less restrictive than in late-Victorian Britain, and the pursuit of pleasure and desire is celebrated, the central dilemma continues to resonate: if being good requires self-denial, how do we stop ourselves from being led into temptation and choosing evil?

7: Essay Writing Checklist

As you read, check how many of the recommendations below are followed by the essay. Then, use the checklist to help you write your own essay.

Remember that these are *recommendations* from an experienced teacher, not *requirements*. Allow them to help and guide you, but don't allow them to restrict you; if you have a different idea and feel confident about it, then give it a go!

- [ ] Use wording of question in answer – "Stevenson presents."
- [ ] Use Intro and Conclusion to help structure essay as argument.
- [ ] Use topic sentences to open each main paragraph.
- [ ] Close focus on extract.
- [ ] Focus on elsewhere in the novel.
- [ ] Use short, precise quotations to support interpretations.
- [ ] Close analysis of language.
- [ ] Close analysis of form.
- [ ] Close analysis of text structure.
- [ ] Refer to effect on reader.
- [ ] Use relevant subject terminology.
- [ ] Connect to context when text was written, where relevant: late-Victorian era.
- [ ] Connect to context when text is set, where relevant: late-Victorian era.
- [ ] Connect to literary context, where relevant: history of the Gothic genre.
- [ ] Connect to original and 21st century audience context, where relevant.
- [ ] Focus on minor character(s), where relevant.
- [ ] Use accurate spelling, punctuation and grammar.
- [ ] Write c450-c750 words.

8: Disturbing and threatening

Read the following extract from Chapter 8 (The Last Night) of *The Strange Case of Dr Jekyll and Mr Hyde* and then answer the question that follows.

In this extract, Utterson and Poole go to Dr Jekyll's house because they are worried about him.

> It was a wild, cold, seasonable night of March, with a pale moon, lying on her back as though the wind had tilted her, and a flying wrack of the most diaphanous and lawny texture. The wind made talking difficult, and flecked the blood into the face. It seemed to have swept the streets unusually bare of passengers, besides; for Mr. Utterson thought he had never seen that part of London so deserted. He could have wished it otherwise; never in his life had he been conscious of so sharp a wish to see and touch his fellow-creatures; for, struggle as he might, there was borne in upon his mind a crushing anticipation of calamity. The square, when they got there, was all full of wind and dust, and the thin trees in the garden were lashing themselves along the railing. Poole, who had kept all the way a pace or two ahead, now pulled up in the middle of the pavement, and, in spite of the biting weather, took off his hat and mopped his brow with a red pocket-handkerchief. But for all the hurry of his coming, these were not the dews of exertion that he wiped away, but the moisture of some strangling anguish; for his face was white, and his voice, when he spoke, harsh and broken.
>
> "Well, sir," he said, "here we are, and God grant there be nothing wrong."
>
> "Amen, Poole," said the lawyer.
>
> Thereupon the servant knocked in a very guarded manner; the door was opened on the chain; and a voice asked from within, "Is that you, Poole?"
>
> "It's all right," said Poole. "Open the door."
>
> The hall, when they entered it, was brightly lighted up; the fire was built high; and about the hearth the whole of the servants, men and women, stood huddled together like a flock of sheep. At the sight of Mr. Utterson, the

> housemaid broke into hysterical whimpering; and the cook, crying out "Bless God! it's Mr. Utterson," ran forward as if to take him in her arms.
>
> "What, what? Are you all here?" said the lawyer peevishly. "Very irregular, very unseemly; your master would be far from pleased."
>
> "They're all afraid," said Poole.

Starting with this extract, explore how Stevenson uses settings to create a disturbing and threatening atmosphere.

Write about:

- how Stevenson uses settings in this extract
- how Stevenson uses settings to create a disturbing and threatening atmosphere in the novel as a whole

8: The Essay

In *Jekyll and Hyde*, Stevenson suffuses his settings with a disturbing and threatening atmosphere. London is described as a brooding place, full of secrets, emphasising Hyde's depravity. Most of the events portrayed happen at night and the few interior settings we see are lit by flickering firelight, creating dramatic, disturbing contrasts between darkness and light that highlight the battle between good and evil at the heart of the story. Stevenson's London is not a place of commerce and culture but a warren of slums and decay where threat, and Mr Hyde, lurk around every corner.

In the extract, Stevenson uses settings to highlight an ever-present sense of threat. Poole and Utterson pass through a deserted city lit by a "pale moon, lying on her back as though the wind had tilted her." (p27) This simile suggests that the wind is actively seeking to create disorder, foreshadowing the disorder that the characters are about to witness. Subsequently, the atmosphere becomes even more threatening when the trees are described as "lashing themselves along the railing." (p27) This eerie pathetic fallacy suggests that the trees are actively choosing to hurt themselves. Subsequently, the interior of Jekyll's house, though brightly lit, only serves to deepen the sense of threat. The servants, clearly scared behind a chained door, appeal in direct speech to God while Utterson brusquely criticises their "irregular" and "unseemly" (p28) behaviour. This shows that Utterson is disturbed by the servants' unusual behaviour, suggesting that, like many late-Victorians, he believes there is an order to society that must be upheld; for Utterson, it seems, the servants' breaking of rules is as disturbing as Dr Jekyll's transgressions.

Earlier in the novel, Stevenson creates a disturbing and threatening atmosphere by presenting London as a gothic landscape of darkness and neglect. Near Hyde's house, London is presented as being dark in the daytime as the wind, "charging and routing," (p17) tries to defeat a dense fog. The personification of the wind, and the military metaphors, suggest a tense battle between darkness and light – a battle that darkness is winning – perhaps reflecting a similar moral battle for Dr Jekyll's soul. Utterson is then presented as disturbed by the area, considering it to be "like a district of some city in a nightmare." (p17) The simile imparts a sense of threat to the scene, suggesting that Utterson is arriving at a place of danger. Utterson is then presented as being highly disturbed by "blackguardly" (p17) scenes of impoverished women out for "a morning glass." (p17) Utterson is clearly disturbed by Dr Jekyll, a multi-millionaire (in today's money),[8] choosing to befriend someone living in this place, surrounded by foreign alcoholics. As was common among wealthy Victorians, poverty is understood by Utterson as a moral failing rather than an institutional failure or a lack of charity, and he condemns Dr Jekyll for the disturbing habit of consorting with people he believes to be beneath them both.

Towards the end of the novel, Stevenson reveals Dr Jekyll's rooms to be an eerie, disturbing place of bizarre scientific experimentation. The approach to Dr Jekyll's cabinet is via an operating theatre, previously used for medical teaching, that now lies "gaunt and silent." (p19) The personification suggests the room itself has fallen ill, wasting away, echoing Jekyll's own physical transformation and his decisive turn away from the benevolence of practising medicine to his malevolent actions as Hyde. Later, Dr Jekyll's cabinet is presented as eerily calm. The fire is "chattering," (p33) and the kettle is "singing" (p33), the personification suggesting that the room is a friendly, happy place while creating a disturbing contrast with the "contorted...twitching" (p33) body of Hyde. On closer inspection, however, Utterson and Poole realise that the cabinet is, in fact, a place of evil and threat. They gaze into a mirror "with an involuntary horror" (p34) and see reflected there "the fire sparkling in a hundred repetitions." (p34) The imagery suggests hellfire and the mirror appears to enable the characters to see past the apparent gentility of the setting, and of Dr Jekyll, and to come close to understanding the horrifying truth – that this is a place of disturbing scientific experimentation, a place of sin.

Thus, Stevenson uses the settings in the novel to create a disturbing and threatening atmosphere. London is presented as a gothic city of darkness where threat thrives in every crumbling alley. Nature is disordered and threatening, the oppressive fog creating a sense of mystery and, of course, allowing Hyde to feed his depraved desires undetected. Dr Jekyll's cabinet, which should be a place of benevolent wisdom, is instead a disturbing place of unknown concoctions. Ultimately, the sense of threat never fully dissipates – Stevenson never lets the sun rise – and readers are left with the disturbing sense that the threat is still out there, somewhere.

8: Essay Writing Checklist

As you read, check how many of the recommendations below are followed by the essay. Then, use the checklist to help you write your own essay.

Remember that these are *recommendations* from an experienced teacher, not *requirements*. Allow them to help and guide you, but don't allow them to restrict you; if you have a different idea and feel confident about it, then give it a go!

- [ ] Use wording of question in answer – "Stevenson presents."
- [ ] Use Intro and Conclusion to help structure essay as argument.
- [ ] Use topic sentences to open each main paragraph.
- [ ] Close focus on extract.
- [ ] Focus on elsewhere in the novel.
- [ ] Use short, precise quotations to support interpretations.
- [ ] Close analysis of language.
- [ ] Close analysis of form.
- [ ] Close analysis of text structure.
- [ ] Refer to effect on reader.
- [ ] Use relevant subject terminology.
- [ ] Connect to context when text was written, where relevant: late-Victorian era.
- [ ] Connect to context when text is set, where relevant: late-Victorian era.
- [ ] Connect to literary context, where relevant: history of the Gothic genre.
- [ ] Connect to original and 21st century audience context, where relevant.
- [ ] Focus on minor character(s), where relevant.
- [ ] Use accurate spelling, punctuation and grammar.
- [ ] Write c450-c750 words.

9: Duality of man

Read the following extract from Chapter 10 (Henry Jekyll's Full Statement of the Case) of *The Strange Case of Dr Jekyll and Mr Hyde* and then answer the question that follows.

In this extract, Jekyll explains his theory of the 'duality of man.'

> It chanced that the direction of my scientific studies, which led wholly towards the mystic and the transcendental, reacted and shed a strong light on this consciousness of the perennial war among my members. With every day, and from both sides of my intelligence, the moral and the intellectual, I thus drew steadily nearer to that truth, by whose partial discovery I have been doomed to such a dreadful shipwreck: that man is not truly one, but truly two. I say two, because the state of my own knowledge does not pass beyond that point. Others will follow, others will outstrip me on the same lines; and I hazard the guess that man will be ultimately known for a mere polity of multifarious, incongruous and independent denizens. I, for my part, from the nature of my life, advanced infallibly in one direction and in one direction only. It was on the moral side, and in my own person, that I learned to recognise the thorough and primitive duality of man; I saw that, of the two natures that contended in the field of my consciousness, even if I could rightly be said to be either, it was only because I was radically both; and from an early date, even before the course of my scientific discoveries had begun to suggest the most naked possibility of such a miracle, I had learned to dwell with pleasure, as a beloved daydream, on the thought of the separation of these elements. If each, I told myself, could be housed in separate identities, life would be relieved of all that was unbearable; the unjust might go his way, delivered from the aspirations and remorse of his more upright twin; and the just could walk steadfastly and securely on his upward path, doing the good things in which he found his pleasure, and no longer exposed to disgrace and penitence by the hands of this extraneous evil. It was the curse of mankind that these incongruous faggots were thus bound together—that in the agonised womb of consciousness, these polar twins should be continuously struggling. How, then were they dissociated?

Starting with this extract, explore how Stevenson presents the 'duality of man' in *The Strange Case of Dr Jekyll and Mr Hyde*.

Write about:
- how Stevenson presents the 'duality of man' in this extract
- how Stevenson presents the 'duality of man' in the novel as a whole.

9: The Essay

In *Jekyll and Hyde*, Stevenson presents Dr Jekyll investigating his belief that every human has good and evil within them and that, through scientific experiment, the differing personalities can be liberated from each other's control. This leads to the creation of Mr Hyde who is presented as renouncing all self-control and terrorising the innocent inhabitants of London. The other characters are presented as good people, trying hard to disrupt Mr Hyde's campaign of depravity. Stevenson suggests that they too are 'dual' in nature but repress any evil inclinations through pious self-denial, a self-denial that Dr Jekyll emphatically rejects.

In the extract, Stevenson presents Dr Jekyll's confession of his aspiration to separate his good and evil sides. He characterises the troubled co-habitation of good and evil within him as a "perennial war." (p42) The metaphor suggests that good and evil do battle within each person, and also suggests that the battle could be won, with one vanquishing the other. Dr Jekyll argues that this 'truth' reveals the "primitive duality of man." (p42) This suggests that he believes human 'duality' has existed since the earliest humans and lives on, hidden under a veil of civilisation but ready to break free. Stevenson presents Dr Jekyll's motivation for liberating evil from the bounds of morality: he believes it to be a "curse" that the "polar twins," (p43) good and evil, struggle in "the agonised womb of consciousness." (p43) The pregnancy metaphor suggests that Dr Jekyll believes that our identity is not a solid, unchanging phenomenon but instead our mind can give birth to other "multifarious" (p42) identities, including evil ones. From a twenty-first century perspective, Dr Jekyll's conjecture does not appear shocking as post-modern theories argue that we are able to 'perform' multiple versions of our 'selves' in a world of ever-changing narratives. However, to Victorians, this apparent repudiation of rigid beliefs about human nature, would have been profoundly shocking.

Earlier in the novel, Stevenson presents the result of Dr Jekyll's research into the duality of man, Hyde. Utterson's first encounter with Hyde leads him to describe Hyde as "troglodytic" and a "foul soul" marked by "Satan." (p12) This suggests that Jekyll's evil persona is an 'unevolved' cave-dweller, a disturbing primitive human, in league with the devil, with immoral, 'uncivilised' urges. Hyde's disturbing behaviour is further emphasised by Enfield who witnesses Hyde, "like some damned Juggernaut," (p5) trampling over a young girl. The simile others Hyde, associating him with a Hindu festival and suggesting that he is somehow exotic and dangerous, a non-Christian interloper in a generally Christian society. Later, Hyde is presented as killing Sir Danvers Carew "with ape-like fury." (p16) The simile implies that Hyde is something inhuman or perhaps an unevolved human, reflecting the late-Victorian fascination with Darwin's theory of evolution, again suggesting that Hyde is more 'primitive' than 'civilised' humans. Thus, having unbound evil from good, Dr Jekyll realises he has created humanity's only "pure evil" (p45) person and seems to celebrate it.

However, though evil roams free, Stevenson presents characters striving for good to triumph. For example, Utterson is presented as leading an "austere" (p3) self-denying life, taking very seriously the "stringent obligations" (p25) of his profession. Thus, Utterson's solution to his 'duality' is a commitment to a quiet, dull life. Paradoxically, Utterson's heroic resistance of the temptations of evil leads to evil: respecting Lanyon's injunction not to read his document until after Dr Jekyll's death means he misses an opportunity to save Dr Jekyll. The challenge of 'duality' is explored further through Jekyll's efforts to embrace goodness. Jekyll describes his good life as that of a "discontented doctor" (p49) living a life of "severity." (p49) Again, a good life is presented as harsh and unattractive compared to the "secret pleasures" (p49) of evil. Jekyll subsequently describes himself as a "sinner" (p50) who, attempting to "redeem the past," "fell before the assaults of temptation." (p50) The metaphor presents the two sides of Dr Jekyll's dual identity at war – the good besieged and defeated by evil. Jekyll's language echoes the story of The Fall that Christians believe unleashed evil into the world.[9] He sees himself as irredeemable, another Adam, who failed to resist the temptation of knowledge and is therefore damned for eternity.

Thus, Stevenson presents characters struggling with their 'duality'. Dr Jekyll's decision to liberate evil leads, predictably, to violence and horror. The other characters' imperviousness to the temptations of evil is presented as an austere suppression of desires and feelings in favour of following strict rules, reflecting late-Victorian piety that celebrated such self-denial. Ultimately, Stevenson argues that, though there may be a good and an evil side to everyone's personality, we all have the ability to choose which will triumph.

9: Essay Writing Checklist

As you read, check how many of the recommendations below are followed by the essay. Then, use the checklist to help you write your own essay.

Remember that these are *recommendations* from an experienced teacher, not *requirements*. Allow them to help and guide you, but don't allow them to restrict you; if you have a different idea and feel confident about it, then give it a go!

- ☐ Use wording of question in answer – "Stevenson presents."
- ☐ Use Intro and Conclusion to help structure essay as argument.
- ☐ Use topic sentences to open each main paragraph.
- ☐ Close focus on extract.
- ☐ Focus on elsewhere in the novel.
- ☐ Use short, precise quotations to support interpretations.
- ☐ Close analysis of language.
- ☐ Close analysis of form.
- ☐ Close analysis of text structure.
- ☐ Refer to effect on reader.
- ☐ Use relevant subject terminology.
- ☐ Connect to context when text was written, where relevant: late-Victorian era.
- ☐ Connect to context when text is set, where relevant: late-Victorian era.
- ☐ Connect to literary context, where relevant: history of the Gothic genre.
- ☐ Connect to original and 21st century audience context, where relevant.
- ☐ Focus on minor character(s), where relevant.
- ☐ Use accurate spelling, punctuation and grammar.
- ☐ Write c450-c750 words.

10: Investigation

Read the following extract from Chapter 6 (Remarkable Incident of Dr Lanyon) of *The Strange Case of Dr Jekyll and Mr Hyde* and then answer the question that follows.

In this extract, Utterson receives a document from Dr Lanyon.

> A week afterwards Dr Lanyon took to his bed, and in something less than a fortnight he was dead. The night after the funeral, at which he had been sadly affected, Utterson locked the door of his business room, and sitting there by the light of a melancholy candle, drew out and set before him an envelope addressed by the hand and sealed with the seal of his dead friend. "PRIVATE: for the hands of G. J. Utterson ALONE, and in case of his predecease *to be destroyed unread*," so it was emphatically superscribed; and the lawyer dreaded to behold the contents. "I have buried one friend to-day," he thought: "what if this should cost me another?" And then he condemned the fear as a disloyalty, and broke the seal. Within there was another enclosure, likewise sealed, and marked upon the cover as "not to be opened till the death or disappearance of Dr Henry Jekyll." Utterson could not trust his eyes. Yes, it was disappearance; here again, as in the mad will which he had long ago restored to its author, here again were the idea of a disappearance and the name of Henry Jekyll bracketed. But in the will, that idea had sprung from the sinister suggestion of the man Hyde; it was set there with a purpose all too plain and horrible. Written by the hand of Lanyon, what should it mean? A great curiosity came on the trustee, to disregard the prohibition and dive at once to the bottom of these mysteries; but professional honour and faith to his dead friend were stringent obligations; and the packet slept in the inmost corner of his private safe.

Starting with this extract, explore how Stevenson presents Utterson's investigation of the connection between Dr Jekyll and Mr Hyde in *The Strange Case of Dr Jekyll and Mr Hyde*.

Write about:
- how Stevenson presents Utterson's investigation of the connection between Dr Jekyll and Mr Hyde in this extract
- how Stevenson presents Utterson's investigation of the connection between Dr Jekyll and Mr Hyde in the novel as a whole.

10: The Essay

In *Jekyll and Hyde*, Stevenson presents Utterson trying, but failing, to solve the strange case of Dr Jekyll and Mr Hyde. Utterson believes that Hyde is blackmailing Dr Jekyll for his considerable wealth and, given that Hyde is the main beneficiary of Dr Jekyll's will, Utterson is also concerned that Hyde will kill Dr Jekyll in order to inherit more quickly. However, Utterson's rational methodical approach cannot unlock the truth and it requires Dr Jekyll's confession to reveal that Jekyll and Hyde are the same person.

In the extract, Stevenson presents Utterson receiving some vital evidence for his investigation. Grieving the death of Dr Lanyon, Utterson sits to examine the evidence by "the light of a melancholy candle." (p24) The pathetic fallacy suggests that even the candle is sharing Utterson's grief and implies the room is only dimly lit, perhaps a reflection of Utterson's own lack of clarity about Dr Jekyll. Utterson methodically opens and examines the document but cannot "trust his eyes" (p24) when he realises that Lanyon has predicted the possible future disappearance of Dr Jekyll and arranged for a document to be opened in that circumstance. Utterson struggles to understand why such an unlikely possibility has been prepared for and he is curious about the document but remembers his "professional honour" and the "stringent obligations" (p25) of his connection to Lanyon and leaves it unread. This paradoxically shows Utterson choosing to be moral by following the rules but, inadvertently, by not reading Lanyon's proof of Dr Jekyll and Mr Hyde's connection, allowing Hyde's reign of terror to continue.

Earlier in the novel, Stevenson presents Utterson's first attempts at understanding the bizarre relationship between Dr Jekyll and Mr Hyde. His first instinct after hearing Enfield's horrifying recount of Hyde's nocturnal criminality is to read Dr Jekyll's will and wonder again why Hyde is named as Dr Jekyll's beneficiary, commenting that he'd previously "thought it was madness" but now "fear[s] it is disgrace." (p8) This shows Utterson's methodical train of thought, weighing evidence and re-evaluating previous judgments, but also shows his sense of morality and social decorum as the idea that his upstanding friend could be associated with "a fiend," (p8) is very troubling for him. This leads to a restless night's sleep as Utterson is attacked by nightmares conjured by his "enslaved" (p9) imagination. The metaphor shockingly suggests that Utterson is unwillingly compelled to ponder the strange case and repeatedly imagine the screaming children left in Hyde's destructive wake. Stevenson then presents Utterson's horrified first impression of Hyde. He describes Hyde as "troglodytic" and a "foul soul" marked by "Satan," (p12) suggesting that he is an 'unevolved' cave-dweller, a disturbing primitive human, in league with the devil, with immoral, 'uncivilised' urges. These visceral impressions reflect late-Victorian ideas about religion and morality and show, again, that Utterson's investigation is hampered by his adherence to social convention from understanding the incredible truth.

Later, Stevenson presents Utterson being misled by Dr Jekyll and attempting to interpret yet more written evidence. After Hyde kills Sir Danvers Carew, Dr Jekyll claims that Hyde will "never more be heard of." (p19) Utterson is understandably wary of Jekyll's certainty, and it is only later we learn that this is the beginning of Dr Jekyll's attempt to wean himself off the potion. Utterson is misled again by a letter, purportedly written by Hyde, that proclaims that Hyde will no longer threaten Dr Jekyll, his "benefactor." (p20) This document causes Utterson to re-assess his prior suspicions and to believe that Jekyll's connection to Hyde was one of charity, not of blackmail. However, Stevenson then presents Utterson inspecting the letter more closely, with the help of his head clerk, a handwriting expert, who notices the "quaint" (p22) similarity between Jekyll and Hyde's handwriting. This strangely hedged adjective is repeated, suggesting that Utterson is resorting to euphemism, unwilling to speak aloud, or even fully accept, the horrifying truth, as his mind races and his "blood [runs] cold." (p22) The metaphor reinforces the horror Utterson is feeling, suggesting once again that Utterson has a visceral understanding of the strange case but his rational personality cannot accept this, so he is never successful in uncovering the truth'

Thus, Stevenson presents a failed investigation. Utterson, intrigued, horrified and motivated by genuine care for his friend seeks evidence, asks questions and examines documents. A rational man of the law, he doggedly pursues real-world explanations for Hyde's connection with Dr Jekyll. However, Dr Jekyll's confession reveals the truth and Utterson realises too late that this was a story of bizarre scientific experimentation, depravity and evil, far beyond anything that the conventional Utterson could ever have imagined.

10: Essay Writing Checklist

As you read, check how many of the recommendations below are followed by the essay. Then, use the checklist to help you write your own essay.

Remember that these are *recommendations* from an experienced teacher, not *requirements*. Allow them to help and guide you, but don't allow them to restrict you; if you have a different idea and feel confident about it, then give it a go!

- ☐ Use wording of question in answer – "Stevenson presents."
- ☐ Use Intro and Conclusion to help structure essay as argument.
- ☐ Use topic sentences to open each main paragraph.
- ☐ Close focus on extract.
- ☐ Focus on elsewhere in the novel.
- ☐ Use short, precise quotations to support interpretations.
- ☐ Close analysis of language.
- ☐ Close analysis of form.
- ☐ Close analysis of text structure.
- ☐ Refer to effect on reader.
- ☐ Use relevant subject terminology.
- ☐ Connect to context when text was written, where relevant: late-Victorian era.
- ☐ Connect to context when text is set, where relevant: late-Victorian era.
- ☐ Connect to literary context, where relevant: history of the Gothic genre.
- ☐ Connect to original and 21st century audience context, where relevant.
- ☐ Focus on minor character(s), where relevant.
- ☐ Use accurate spelling, punctuation and grammar.
- ☐ Write c450-c750 words.

11: Friendship

Read the following extract from Chapter 3 (Dr Jekyll was quite at Ease) of *The Strange Case of Dr Jekyll and Mr Hyde* and then answer the question that follows.

In this extract, Utterson and Dr Jekyll discuss Dr Jekyll's connection to Mr Hyde.

> "Jekyll," said Utterson, "you know me: I am a man to be trusted. Make a clean breast of this in confidence; and I make no doubt I can get you out of it."
>
> "My good Utterson," said the doctor, "this is very good of you, this is downright good of you, and I cannot find words to thank you in. I believe you fully; I would trust you before any man alive, ay, before myself, if I could make the choice; but indeed it isn't what you fancy; it is not as bad as that; and just to put your good heart at rest, I will tell you one thing: the moment I choose, I can be rid of Mr Hyde. I give you my hand upon that; and I thank you again and again; and I will just add one little word, Utterson, that I'm sure you'll take in good part: this is a private matter, and I beg of you to let it sleep."
>
> Utterson reflected a little, looking in the fire.
>
> "I have no doubt you are perfectly right," he said at last, getting to his feet.
>
> "Well, but since we have touched upon this business, and for the last time I hope," continued the doctor, "there is one point I should like you to understand. I have really a very great interest in poor Hyde. I know you have seen him; he told me so; and I fear he was rude. But I do sincerely take a great, a very great interest in that young man; and if I am taken away, Utterson, I wish you to promise me that you will bear with him and get his rights for him. I think you would, if you knew all; and it would be a weight off my mind if you would promise."
>
> "I can't pretend that I shall ever like him," said the lawyer.
>
> "I don't ask that," pleaded Jekyll, laying his hand upon the other's arm; "I only ask for justice; I only ask you to help him for my sake, when I am no longer here."
>
> Utterson heaved an irrepressible sigh. "Well," said he, "I promise."

Starting with this extract, explore how Stevenson presents friendship in *The Strange Case of Dr Jekyll and Mr Hyde*.

Write about:
- how Stevenson presents friendship in this extract
- how Stevenson presents friendship in the novel as a whole.

11: The Essay

In *Jekyll and Hyde*, Stevenson presents a group of professional gentlemen working hard to help one of their friends who, they believe, has fallen under the spell of an evil murderer. Utterson gathers evidence and tracks down the person he believes to be the culprit: Hyde. However, Dr Jekyll, whom we eventually learn is Mr Hyde, misleads Utterson, taking advantage of his friendship and manipulating his sense of honour in an effort to conceal the truth. Stevenson shows how friends can be a help in times of need but also shows how friendships can be exploited, and fracture, in an atmosphere of lies and suspicion.

In the extract, Stevenson presents how Dr Jekyll uses Utterson's loyalty as a good friend to obtain a promise. Utterson shows his faith in ideals of friendship by declaring that he has "no doubt" (p14) he can solve Jekyll's problems as long as Jekyll makes "a clean breast" (p14) of what he knows. The metaphor shows that Utterson sees lies and evasiveness as sullying his friends' conscience and suggests that he innocently believes that honesty will solve even the most intractable problem. However, Dr Jekyll chooses instead to lie by omission. He declares he "can be rid of Mr Hyde" (p15) any moment he chooses and offers his handshake as proof of his word. His use of the gesture, associated with verbal contracts between good friends who believes themselves to be 'men of their word', helps to persuade Utterson, an honourable Victorian gentleman, to reluctantly agree to let the matter drop. Stevenson then presents Dr Jekyll extracting a promise from his friend to "bear with" the "young man" (p15) Hyde, in the case of Dr Jekyll's death. Utterson, trapped by his principles, and his loyalty to his friend, agrees to do so, very reluctantly, the long pauses as he makes his decision indicative of his qualms. Stevenson shows that Utterson's friendship for Jekyll will extend even beyond death.

Earlier in the novel, Stevenson shows how a close-knit group of friends aim to live hardworking moral lives. Utterson is presented as leading an "austere" (p3) self-denying life, in which the "singularly dull" (p3) walk with his relative, and friend, Enfield, is the "chief jewel" (p3) of his week. The metaphor emphasises how prized this weekly ritual is for the two friends who, unlike Dr Jekyll, do not pursue depravity as a leisure activity. Later, we see Dr Jekyll displaying a "sincere and warm affection" (p14) for Utterson, basking in his "rich silence." (p14) Their relationship is built on sobriety and quiet rationality and is presented by Stevenson as an ideal of friendship, clearly antithetical to the grotesque antics of Dr Jekyll's evil persona. Later, Stevenson presents Utterson's relationship with his head clerk, Guest, as respectful and friendly. Unusually for Utterson, wine is drunk, which causes him, "insensibly," to "melt" (p21) and share his suspicions about Dr Jekyll with his employee. The metaphor emphasises a rare moment in the novel where Utterson condescends, showing respect for those below him in the social hierarchy, caused perhaps by the dissolving power of alcohol. Thus, Stevenson shows how, for Utterson and the other apparently unmarried men in his circle, friendship is of the utmost importance, subject to a code of honour and loyalty that, unfortunately for them, Dr Jekyll undermines.

Elsewhere, Stevenson presents how friendship can break down when Dr Jekyll's friends criticise his scientific experimentation. Dr Lanyon is presented as an old but estranged friend of Dr Jekyll. He rejects Dr Jekyll's research interests as "unscientific balderdash" (p9) while Dr Jekyll rejects Dr Lanyon as a "hide-bound pedant." (p14) Their dispute creates an antithesis: Dr Lanyon is in favour of closely following scientific rules while Dr Jekyll is in favour of rejecting old-fashioned ideas and petty detail. Though this portrays Dr Jekyll favourably (especially to a twenty-first century audience) as a free-thinker, generating new knowledge, readers know that Dr Jekyll's free-thinking is highly destructive. Later, Dr Jekyll's internal debate hinges on his fear of being cast out of polite society and living "despised and friendless" (p48) and his enjoyment of the "leaping pulses" and "liberty" (p49) of becoming Hyde. This suggests that friendship is a bind, with obligations and rules that Hyde would happily shake off but Dr Jekyll seeks to retain. Ultimately, of course, Dr Jekyll succumbs to the temptation of being Hyde, rejecting the model of loyal, moral friendship set by Utterson.

Thus, Stevenson presents friendship amongst Victorian professional gentlemen as based on loyalty, honour, sobriety and discretion. Their lives aren't, by twenty-first century standards, fun, but Stevenson suggests that moral austerity is a better choice than dissipation. Accordingly, Utterson's decision to help Dr Jekyll is born of friendship, but Dr Jekyll's decision to become, repeatedly, Mr Hyde is presented as a rejection of such friendship in favour of a depraved individualism that upends social convention and leads to horrifying consequences.

11: Essay Writing Checklist

As you read, check how many of the recommendations below are followed by the essay. Then, use the checklist to help you write your own essay.

Remember that these are *recommendations* from an experienced teacher, not *requirements*. Allow them to help and guide you, but don't allow them to restrict you; if you have a different idea and feel confident about it, then give it a go!

- [ ] Use wording of question in answer – "Stevenson presents."
- [ ] Use Intro and Conclusion to help structure essay as argument.
- [ ] Use topic sentences to open each main paragraph.
- [ ] Close focus on extract.
- [ ] Focus on elsewhere in the novel.
- [ ] Use short, precise quotations to support interpretations.
- [ ] Close analysis of language.
- [ ] Close analysis of form.
- [ ] Close analysis of text structure.
- [ ] Refer to effect on reader.
- [ ] Use relevant subject terminology.
- [ ] Connect to context when text was written, where relevant: late-Victorian era.
- [ ] Connect to context when text is set, where relevant: late-Victorian era.
- [ ] Connect to literary context, where relevant: history of the Gothic genre.
- [ ] Connect to original and 21st century audience context, where relevant.
- [ ] Focus on minor character(s), where relevant.
- [ ] Use accurate spelling, punctuation and grammar.
- [ ] Write c450-c750 words.

12: Science

Read the following extract from Chapter 10 (Henry Jekyll's Full Statement of the Case) of *The Strange Case of Dr Jekyll and Mr Hyde* and then answer the question that follows.

In this extract, Jekyll describes his first experience of taking the potion.

> I knew well that I risked death; for any drug that so potently controlled and shook the very fortress of identity, might, by the least scruple of an overdose or at the least inopportunity in the moment of exhibition, utterly blot out that immaterial tabernacle which I looked to it to change. But the temptation of a discovery so singular and profound at last overcame the suggestions of alarm. I had long since prepared my tincture; I purchased at once, from a firm of wholesale chemists, a large quantity of a particular salt which I knew, from my experiments, to be the last ingredient required; and late one accursed night, I compounded the elements, watched them boil and smoke together in the glass, and when the ebullition had subsided, with a strong glow of courage, drank off the potion.
>
> The most racking pangs succeeded: a grinding in the bones, deadly nausea, and a horror of the spirit that cannot be exceeded at the hour of birth or death. Then these agonies began swiftly to subside, and I came to myself as if out of a great sickness. There was something strange in my sensations, something indescribably new and, from its very novelty, incredibly sweet. I felt younger, lighter, happier in body; within I was conscious of a heady recklessness, a current of disordered sensual images running like a millrace in my fancy, a solution of the bonds of obligation, an unknown but not an innocent freedom of the soul.

Starting with this extract, explore how Stevenson presents the effects of Dr Jekyll's scientific experimentation in *The Strange Case of Dr Jekyll and Mr Hyde*.

Write about:
- how Stevenson presents the effects of Dr Jekyll's scientific experimentation in this extract
- how Stevenson presents the effects of Dr Jekyll's scientific experimentation in the novel as a whole.

12: The Essay

In *Jekyll and Hyde*, Stevenson presents the horrifying consequences of Dr Jekyll's scientific experimentation. Rather than pursuing science for benevolent ends, Dr Jekyll's experiments lead to the production of a potion that transforms him into Hyde, who rampages through London leaving death and destruction in his wake. Dr Jekyll is presented as rejecting old-fashioned scientific ideas in favour of creative liberty and the 'joy' of depraved experimentation. Ultimately, however, Stevenson shows that Dr Jekyll's liberty and 'joy' lead him only to his doom.

In the extract, Stevenson presents how Dr Jekyll's potion causes a horrifying transformation. Dr Jekyll is aware of the potential harms caused by shaking the "fortress of identity" (p43) and destroying its "tabernacle." (p43) The mixed metaphors (military and religious) present Dr Jekyll's identity as both a place that needs heavy protection from attack and a place where God is believed to dwell.[10] Readers may wonder why, if identity is such an impenetrable, holy concept, Dr Jekyll seeks to dissolve it. His motivations seem muddled, even evil, and the presentation of the potion that "boil[s] and smoke[s]" (p43), redolent of hellfire, emphasises our sense that only "horror" (p43) can come from this experiment. Indeed, the potion immediately causes intense physical and psychological pain but, once the pain subsides, Dr Jekyll describes "a solution of the bonds of obligation" and a "freedom of the soul." (p44) The potion is presented as melting away the web of rules and convention that connect Dr Jekyll to society; he no longer feels compelled to behave in the expected manner, that of a Victorian gentleman. Maybe Dr Jekyll's experiment, though dangerous, has produced a positive effect: freedom.

Readers, of course, know the truth as, earlier in the novel, Stevenson presents the horrifying effect of this experiment: Hyde. Enfield narrates how Hyde, "like some damned Juggernaut," (p5) tramples over a young girl. The simile others Hyde, associating him with a Hindu festival and suggesting that this product of Dr Jekyll's experiment is somehow exotic and dangerous, a non-Christian outsider in a generally Christian society. Later, another brutal effect of Jekyll's experiment is presented when Hyde is shown killing Sir Danvers Carew "with ape-like fury." (p16) The simile presents Hyde as an unevolved human, reflecting the late-Victorian fascination with Darwin's theory of evolution, suggesting that Hyde is more 'primitive' than 'civilised' humans. Stevenson thus suggests that Dr Jekyll's scientific experiment leads only to the freedom to hurt and kill. In fact, Dr Jekyll later reveals that, as Hyde, he thoroughly enjoyed the "liberty" and "glee" (p49) of "depravity" (p46) and, ultimately, lost control of the transformation process. Having attempted to give a veneer of scientific respectability to his 'research', Dr Jekyll now seems to admit that he was driven by a desire to 'go wild'. Readers may well reject Dr Jekyll's justifications for his actions and interpret his scientific experimentation simply as the actions of a wealthy man using his money to attempt to satisfy his lusts undetected.

Elsewhere, Stevenson presents how Dr Jekyll's scientific experimentation causes his friends to express doubts about his behaviour. Dr Lanyon rejects Dr Jekyll's research interests as "unscientific balderdash" (p9) while Dr Jekyll rejects Dr Lanyon as a "hide-bound pedant." (p14) Their dispute creates an antithesis: Dr Lanyon is in favour of closely following scientific rules while Dr Jekyll is in favour of rejecting old-fashioned ideas and petty detail. Though this portrays Dr Jekyll favourably (especially to a twenty-first century audience) as a free-thinker, generating new knowledge, readers, having witnessed the horror of Hyde, know that Dr Jekyll's free-thinking is highly destructive. Stevenson then presents Dr Jekyll attempting to justify his scientific experimentation by hypothesising the "mist-like transience" (p43) of our physical selves. The simile emphasises Dr Jekyll's belief that the human self is not solid but in fact "radically" (p42) dual. From a twenty-first century perspective, Dr Jekyll's conjecture does not appear shocking as post-modern theories argue that we are able to 'perform' multiple versions of our 'selves' in a world of ever-changing narratives. However, Dr Jekyll then argues that our dual natures should be separated to allow this "curse of mankind," (p43) our duality, to be lifted. Thus, Stevenson shows that the effect of Dr Jekyll's scientific experimentation would be a world of radically evil people, unrestrained by their other, more moral, nature.

Thus, Stevenson presents the horrifying and violent effects of Dr Jekyll's scientific experimentation. Moreover, the implications of Dr Jekyll's findings – science should liberate humans from moral goodness to allow us to be truly free – are chilling, and presage later extremist ideologies.[11] Ultimately, Stevenson does not allay any late-Victorian anxieties about the deleterious effects of scientific progress so, as long as individuals are driven to push the boundaries of science in the same way Dr Jekyll is, we may always need to be alert to the ways it can be perverted and put to malign use.

12: Essay Writing Checklist

As you read, check how many of the recommendations below are followed by the essay. Then, use the checklist to help you write your own essay.

Remember that these are *recommendations* from an experienced teacher, not *requirements*. Allow them to help and guide you, but don't allow them to restrict you; if you have a different idea and feel confident about it, then give it a go!

- ☐ Use wording of question in answer – "Stevenson presents."
- ☐ Use Intro and Conclusion to help structure essay as argument.
- ☐ Use topic sentences to open each main paragraph.
- ☐ Close focus on extract.
- ☐ Focus on elsewhere in the novel.
- ☐ Use short, precise quotations to support interpretations.
- ☐ Close analysis of language.
- ☐ Close analysis of form.
- ☐ Close analysis of text structure.
- ☐ Refer to effect on reader.
- ☐ Use relevant subject terminology.
- ☐ Connect to context when text was written, where relevant: late-Victorian era.
- ☐ Connect to context when text is set, where relevant: late-Victorian era.
- ☐ Connect to literary context, where relevant: history of the Gothic genre.
- ☐ Connect to original and 21st century audience context, where relevant.
- ☐ Focus on minor character(s), where relevant.
- ☐ Use accurate spelling, punctuation and grammar.
- ☐ Write c450-c750 words.

Appendix 1: How will my essay be assessed?

In your AQA GCSE English Literature exams, the *Jekyll and Hyde* task will count for 19% of your total marks so practising essay writing is absolutely vital and can make a huge difference to your final grades.

How will my essay be assessed?

The exam board will assess your essay by checking to see how far you have met the three Assessment Objectives:

AO1	Read, understand and respond to texts. Students should be able to: • maintain a critical style and develop an informed personal response • use textual references, including quotations, to support and illustrate interpretations.
AO2	Analyse the language, form and structure used by a writer to create meanings and effects, using relevant subject terminology where appropriate.
AO3	Show understanding of the relationships between texts and the contexts in which they were written.

This exam board language, however, can feel a bit technical or vague. After all, what is a "critical style"? Who decides what is "appropriate" and what isn't?

(Answers: a critical style means that your essay should demonstrate its conclusions by using evidence from the text. Don't simply tell the examiner that Hyde is violent; prove it using evidence from the text. And: it is your examiner, ultimately, who will decide what is appropriate and what isn't.)

Rather than answering these questions theoretically, the essays in this book aim to show in practical terms how it's possible to give your examiner what they are looking for, within the time constraints of the exam, whilst showing off the full range of your text knowledge and writing technique.

What makes these essays excellent exam essays?

It is true that there are many ways to organise information in an essay and you, or your teacher, may have different preferences about how to approach writing these essays. The essays in this book reflect my judgement of what is the best approach based on my professional knowledge of what works for my students, my knowledge of what is readily readable by examiners and, perhaps most importantly, my own experience of writing these essays under timed conditions.

The twelve essays here follow a consistent pattern:

- an Introduction paragraph outlining in summary the answer to the essay question.
- three detailed Main Paragraphs offering a critical analysis, first of the extract and subsequently other parts of the novel, providing evidence to back up my answer. These paragraphs also include, where relevant, connections to the text's contexts.
- a final Conclusion paragraph offering a re-statement of the essay answer in summary form with, where relevant, connections to the resonance of the text for modern audiences.

This pattern can be learned and repeated, making it an excellent tool for students. It is achievable under the time constraints of the exam. Finally, the pattern is also clear, readable and, importantly, familiar to examiners which means you are not requiring your examiners to interpret a more muddled, inconsistent structure.

Each essay shows:

- a critical style based on my own understanding of the text.
- textual references (usually short quotations embedded into sentences) used to support interpretations.
- analysis of how Stevenson uses language, form and structure to create meanings and effects.
- relevant subject terminology used where appropriate.
- understanding of the relationship between the text and its contexts (including, where relevant, references to when the text was written and first published, when the text was set and when the text is read in the modern day).

- a range of vocabulary, varied sentence structures, accurate spelling, consistent punctuation and clear grammar.

Finally, these essays are short – around 750 words. The first drafts were written under the same conditions as the ones you will face (50-55 minutes for the AQA exam) and therefore reflect what is possible in such a short time. You may initially find it difficult to write so much detail in such a short space of time, but regular practice will definitely enable you to improve.

Best of luck in your exams!

Appendix 2: Endnotes

1 The use of "juggernaut" in English, both in its literal sense and in its later metaphorical sense, is a result of British (i.e. English, Scottish, Welsh and Irish) contact with Indian religious practice during the early period of British rule in India. For more on the history of this word, see the Oxford University Press (OUP) blog post: https://blog.oup.com/2017/08/origins-juggernaut-jagannath/

2 According to the Bank of England Inflation Calculator, £250,000 in 1886 (when *Jekyll and Hyde* was first published) is worth £24,751,772.67 in 2022.

3 "Behold," "beholdeth," "beholding" and "beheld" appear 1350 times in the Authorized Version of the King James Bible. By comparison, "Jesus" appears 943 times.

4 For example, Nietzsche's 'Übermensch' and his concept of the 'will to power', enthusiastically embraced by Hitler as a philosophical foundation for National Socialism.

5 According to the Bank of England Inflation Calculator, £100 in 1886 (when *Jekyll and Hyde* was first published) is worth £9900.71 in 2022.

6 According to the Bank of England Inflation Calculator, £250,000 in 1886 (when *Jekyll and Hyde* was first published) is worth £24,751,772.67 in 2022.

7 From Genesis 3:22-24: "And the Lord God said, Behold, the man is become as one of us, to know good and evil: and now, lest he put forth his hand, and take also of the tree of life, and eat, and live for ever: therefore the Lord God sent him forth from the garden of Eden, to till the ground from whence he was taken. So he drove out the man."

8 According to the Bank of England Inflation Calculator, £250,000 in 1886 (when *Jekyll and Hyde* was first published) is worth £24,751,772.67 in 2022.

9 From Genesis 3:22-24: "And the Lord God said, Behold, the man is become as one of us, to know good and evil: and now, lest he put forth his hand, and take also of the tree of life, and eat, and live for ever: therefore the Lord God sent him

forth from the garden of Eden, to till the ground from whence he was taken. So he drove out the man."

10 The tabernacle (described in Exodus 25-31) was a tent structure believed by the Israelites to be the earthly dwelling place of God. In Roman Catholic and Orthodox churches, the tabernacle is the locked cupboard in which the Blessed Sacrament (consecrated bread, believed to be the Body of Christ) is kept between services.

11 For example, Nietzsche's 'Übermensch' and his concept of the 'will to power', enthusiastically embraced by Hitler as a philosophical foundation for National Socialism.

Printed in Great Britain
by Amazon